Bibliographical Series
of Supplements to 'British Book News'
on Writers and Their Work

★

GENERAL EDITOR
Bonamy Dobrée

SIR THOMAS BROWNE
from a portrait at St. Peter Mancroft, Norwich

SIR THOMAS BROWNE

by
PETER GREEN

If you cannot have Trogus Pompeius
you must be content with Justin,
and accept this epitome and short
account of things, not having the
large and full narration thereof.
Sir Thomas Browne, *Commonplace Books*

PUBLISHED FOR
THE BRITISH COUNCIL
and the NATIONAL BOOK LEAGUE
by LONGMANS, GREEN & CO.

LONGMANS, GREEN & CO. LTD.
6 & 7 Clifford Street, London W.1
Thibault House, Thibault Square, Cape Town
605–611 Lonsdale Street, Melbourne C.1.

LONGMANS, GREEN & CO. INC.
119 West 40th Street, New York 18

LONGMANS, GREEN & CO.
20 Cranfield Road, Toronto 16

ORIENT LONGMANS PRIVATE LTD.
Calcutta   Bombay   Madras
Delhi Hyderabad Dacca

First published in 1959
© Peter Green, 1959

Printed in Great Britain by Unwin Brothers Limited
Woking and London

CONTENTS

¶ Sir Thomas Browne was born in Cheapside, London, on 19 October 1605. He died on 19 October 1682 in Norwich, and is buried in the Church of St. Peter Mancroft.

I

PHYSIC AND METAPHYSIC

THERE is a peculiarly paradoxical flavour about Sir Thomas Browne's position in English letters. Few writers of his distinction have shown less professional interest in literature as such: what primarily concerned Browne were the twin themes of scientific research and religious exploration. He fell into public authorship by accident; and, with paradoxical irony, he is remembered today less for his experiments in embryology or even his anti-sectarian mysticism than for his unique style. We know that, as Buffon said, *le style c'est l'homme même*; and it is true that Browne's hypnotic, haunting rhythms, the rich texture of his prose, his idiosyncratic vocabulary and imagery are indissolubly bound up with the beliefs he held no less than his professional vocation of medicine. But to read Browne for his style *alone*, as though his work were some religious incantation, the meaning of which had long fallen into oblivion, is to lose the greater part of what he has to offer us. Few prose writers have achieved such associative denseness of texture: the strands which compose his web cannot be separated without damaging the whole.

To recover the atmosphere—emotional no less than intellectual—in which Browne composed his works requires some effort today. Very early the pressing problems which confronted him had changed or were forgotten: Pepys records how already in his day the *Religio Medici* was bracketed with Osborne's cynical *Advice to a Son* and Samuel Butler's *Hudibras*—a collocation which would not, probably, occur to most modern readers—and how 'these three books were the most esteemed and generally cried up *for wit* in the world': an equally surprising verdict. Browne had a talent for making unconscious prophecies about himself: in a letter to his son Thomas he remarked, apropos Lucan: 'I hope you are more taken with the verses than the subject, and rather embrace the expression than the example'. Subsequent generations were not slow to apply the precept to Browne's own work. Yet his style has in the last resort acted as the preservative of his ideas; without it the chances are that he would not now be read at all. It is his pregnant imagery rather than his rational argument which still sends our imagination soaring:

> Those images that yet
> Fresh images beget,

and it is, without doubt, his most famous passages which still have most to offer us today.

Nevertheless, those who have praised Browne most have often understood him least. In his own country he tends to be taken for granted as a harmlessly enjoyable anthology author; the final chapters of *Hydriotaphia* and *The Garden of Cyrus* are known by heart, but seldom analysed. The last full-length study of Browne by an English critic appeared in 1905; since then we have abandoned him to Frenchmen and Americans.

Sir Thomas Browne's life spans the most troubled years of an exceedingly troubled century—troubled politically, socially and above all by the increasing tension between religious transition and scientific discovery. The fugal counter-stresses set up by this tension affected every thinking person, in particular every writer of the period. Browne, Janus-like, faced both ways, at some cost to himself. Sweet reasonableness is never popular with passionate sectarians; and Browne had further to contend with the subtle temptations of his scientific training. 'The Devill, that did but buffet Saint *Paul*, playes mee thinkes at sharpe with me', he wrote. 'There is another man within mee, that's angry with mee, rebukes, commands and dastards mee.' His deep faith was only equalled by his unquenchable experimental curiosity; and it was the two in combination that crystallized his unique mystical prose-poems, as a precipitate forms in the retort from two powerful chemical substances forced together by an external agent. He stood, literally, at the cross-roads of history: past and future fused in him. He could have written at no other time than when he did.

As Professor Willey puts it, 'how to fit a supernaturalist and poetic scripture into the new world-scheme, how to reconcile . . . the whole miraculous structure of Christianity with the new "philosophy" '—this was the problem facing writers so diverse as Bacon and Donne. The tradition of classical Scepticism had been renewed by Gassendi; fresh Aristotelian manuscripts had come to light, which proved exceedingly hard to reconcile with Scholastic doctrine; and hardly was the Anglican rupture with Rome settled when the old cosmology was torn from top to bottom by the theories of Galileo and Copernicus. The possibility that the earth was not, after all, the stable centre of the universe produced a violent psychological shock on all thinking and religious people. Where were the limits of human knowledge to be set? How was belief to be squared with the new revolutionary advances in natural science?

Browne's training as a physician exposed him to such doubts in their most naked form. After a normal English education at Winchester and Pembroke College, Oxford, he left for the Continent in 1630, to pursue his medical studies successively at Montpellier, Padua and Leyden. Montpellier was a half-Catholic, half-Protestant town: the medical school, though backward in anatomy, breathed a liberal atmosphere independent of ecclesiastical authority, and pursued a deliberately revolutionary policy of keeping science and religion in distinct compartments. Harvey had recently graduated from Padua, which was under Venetian protection and in diametrical opposition to Papal control: as a result there was no embargo on clinical dissection, and the anatomy school was the finest in Europe. At Leyden students of all faiths were freely admitted, and the town was, as a result, a hotbed of religious controversy. It was here, in December 1633, that Thomas Browne received his degree as Doctor of Medicine: possibly with a thesis on syphilis, which casts an interesting light on his obsessive imagery relating to death and physical corruption.

In any case it is clear that the new scientific and medical methodology, viewed at close quarters, made an extremely powerful impact on Browne's mind. He, like many of his contemporaries, suffered periods of intense melancholic depression. He clearly came near to losing his faith during his early pursuit of scientific knowledge:

> The Devill played at Chesse with mee, and yeelding a pawne, thought to gaine a Queen of me, taking advantage of my honest endeavours; and whilst I laboured to raise the structure of my reason, hee striv'd to undermine the edifice of my faith.
>
> (*Religio Medici*, Part I, section 19)

Browne found a solution; but it was one more common among Roman Catholics than Anglicans, and tinged with heresy at that: the doctrine known as Fideism.

Fideism was expressed concisely by Pomponazzi a century or more earlier: the Bolognese philosopher defended himself against a charge of heresy by declaring: 'I believe as a Christian what I cannot believe as a philosopher.' The doctrine had plausible classical antecedents, and became popular with writers such as Montaigne, Pico della Mirandola, and Pascal, chiefly through reconciling free intellectual scepticism with an ultimate adherence to religious orthodoxy. It lies at the heart of Sir Thomas Browne's philosophy of life and scientific method. He formulated his principles of thought and belief in his earliest work, the *Religio Medici*, and applied them, diversely, to all his subsequent activities, literary or scientific. The merit of Fideism, from Browne's viewpoint, was that it released his energies for scientific experiment without ever imperilling his religious faith. So sure was he of his ground, in fact, that he could afford to indulge in remarkably trenchant Higher Criticism of the Scriptures. This, together with his profession, is quite enough to explain his reputation, with some of his contemporaries, as an atheist.

Few books, surely, can have so quickly become a classic

yet remained so thoroughly misunderstood as the *Religio Medici*. Its very title appeared a paradox; and certainly its spiritual tolerance and charity—travel had left Browne with a friendly respect for all creeds and customs—must have struck oddly on the ears of that dogmatic and sectarian age:

> I am, I confesse, naturally inclined to that which misguided zeale terms superstition . . . at my devotion I love to use the civility of my knee, my hat, and hand, with all those outward and sensible motions, which may expresse or promote my invisible devotion. . . . At a solemne Procession I have wept abundantly, while my consorts, blinde with opposition and prejudice, have fallen into an excesse of scorne and laughter . . . I could never divide my selfe from any man upon the difference of an opinion, or be angry with his judgement for not agreeing with mee in that, from which perhaps within a few dayes I should dissent my selfe. (*Rel. Med.*, Part I, sections, 3, 6)

On the basis of the *Religio Medici* Browne was not only attacked for atheism, but claimed, with some show of plausibility, both by Catholics and Quakers, as a *de jure* convert.

His approach to Christian dogma is, indeed, somewhat eclectic, not to say muddled. He makes an initial declaration of allegiance to the Church of England; but his subsequent ramblings in Hermetic mysticism, Roman Stoicism, and near-Manichee heresies make it clear that his Anglican faith was infinitely elastic. His favourite doctrine, the Platonic Theory of Ideas, hardly figures in Church of England theology. It should be remembered, however, that the book was conceived as a private summing-up of the author's spiritual and philosophical position after his continental experiences; it was never intended for publication, and only appeared after a text pirated from Browne's manuscript had attracted considerable publicity—mainly through the attentions of Sir Kenelm Digby. Perhaps for this reason it offers a remarkably early example of spiritual self-analysis, unselfconscious to a degree Browne might well have failed to attain if deliberately aiming at an unrestricted public.

In this sense *Religio Medici* possesses, quite apart from its literary or mystical value, much interest considered purely as

an autobiographical document. It is fascinating to learn that
Browne knew six languages, 'beside the *Jargon* and *Patois*
of several provinces'; that he could 'look a whole day with
delight upon a handsome Picture, though it be but of an
Horse'; and that he wished 'we might procreate like trees,
without conjunction'. (He married a year or two later, and
had numerous children; what Dame Dorothy made of this
passage, history does not relate.) His ironic self-appraisal,
however, keeps us perpetually on the alert:

> There is I think no man that apprehends his owne miseries lesse
> than my selfe, and no man that so neerely apprehends anothers. I
> could lose an arme without a teare, and with a few groans, mee
> thinkes, be quartered into pieces; yet can I weepe most seriously at a
> Play, and receive with a true passion, the counterfeit griefes of those
> knowne and professed impostours . . . I thank the goodnesse of God,
> I have no sinnes that want a name; I am not singular in offences;
> my transgressions are Epidemicall, and from the common breath of
> our corruption . . . .   (*Rel. Med.*, Part II, sections 5, 7)

The questions Browne discusses are those most pressing
at the time—the creation or eternity of the world, the nature
of the soul, the truth of God's existence, the rival claims of
faith and reason, the veracity of demons, witches, astrology
and miracles. But his conclusions, and his autobiographical
method (which blends St. Augustine's *Confessions* with the
relaxed temperament of an English Montaigne) are worlds
away from the prevalent theological temper of Anglican
England, more fairly represented by the rational *Ecclesiastical
Polity* of Hooker. It is no coincidence that *Religio Medici*
was better understood, and more fully appreciated, on the
Continent: it is full of continental ideas. Montaigne and
Pascal would have recognized its premises instantly.

Browne's Fideism at one stroke disposes of sectarian
wrangling and, by establishing a double criterion of truth,
opens the door to his beloved scientific experiments:

> As for those wingy mysteries in Divinity, and ayery subtilties of
> Religion, which have unhing'd the braines of better heads, they never
> stretch the *Pia Mater* of mine; mee thinkes there be not impossi-

bilities enough in Religion for an active faith; the deepest mysteries ours containes have not only been illustrated, but maintained, by syllogisme and the rule of reason: I love to lose my selfe in a mystery, to pursue my Reason to an *oh altitudo!* . . . I can answer all the objections of Satan, and my rebellious reason with that odde resolution I learned of *Tertullian, Certum est, quia impossibile est.*

(Part I, section 9)

His faith, in fact, flourishes on mystical paradox: it is hardly surprising that he should relish and repeat the Hermetic definition of God as a circle whose centre is everywhere and whose circumference nowhere.

Those who look for strict consistency in the *Religio Medici* will be disappointed—and ill-advised. The principle of dual reality once established, Browne can relax into his natural temper: what may best be described as religio-scientific romanticism. He ranges like a bee over the whole variegated garden of contemporary thought, sipping where he will, integrating what he needs into his own personal, creative interpretation of the universe. He is at heart a poet: his vision has the direct, symbolic intensity we associate with Vaughan, Traherne, Crashaw, or—above all—Donne, whose famous declaration that 'all divinity is love or wonder' exactly echoes Browne's own attitude. What drew, and continues to draw readers to this idiosyncratic spiritual testament is the creative unity which it imposes on apparently irreconcilable modes of thought; the harmony that can embrace science and faith alike, gather together the scattered, broken symbols and from them strike, clear and complete, the lost music of the spheres.

II

THAT GREAT AMPHIBIUM

Browne's eclectic theology explains why, on the basis of his own utterances, various critics can, with equal plausibility, claim him as a serious scientist, a disciple of Aquinas, or a latter-day Gnostic. (Others, again, have accused him of deliberate duplicity or schizoid thought, the Metaphysical equivalent of Doublethink.) None of these interpretations seems wholly justified; they all approach Browne from a limited and partial viewpoint. 'I attained my purpose', he wrote, 'and came to reach this port by a bare wind, much labour, great paynes and little assistance.' The squaring of his medical with his religious conscience was not achieved by an easy piece of casuistry. One is reminded of Mr. T. S. Eliot's famous remark about the seventeenth century's 'dissociation of sensibility'. In Browne this dissociation can be observed in embryo. His whole creative energy was directed towards the re-integration of already rapidly diverging intellectual and spiritual elements: but it was a vain endeavour. He lived to see his unity of awareness finally destroyed, split apart by the wedge of scientific enquiry unmodified by moral considerations.

Though he knew and approved the work of such pioneers as Descartes, Vesalius the anatomist, and Harvey—whose treatise on the circulation of the blood he valued more highly, he declared, than Columbus' discovery of America— the framework of Browne's thought remained, inevitably, dependent on the old pre-Copernican cosmology. It is no accident that the poet from whom he quotes most often, and who influenced him more than any other literary source except the Bible, is Dante. The great Italian's *Divine Comedy* presented a model of the stable cosmos, mystically conceived, which exactly matched Browne's own temperament: it offered the combination of precise (and often exotic) antiquarianism with a passionate sense of divine order and pattern. Browne might have had the *Paradiso* in mind when he wrote, in the final chapter of *The Garden of Cyrus*: 'All things began in order, so shall they end, and so shall they begin again; according to the ordainer of order and mysticall Mathematicks of the City of Heaven.'

The ultimate responsibility for truth, then, Browne resigns to God; and the old mediaeval Divine Ladder of Being, with its immutable hierarchy, is used by Browne as a pattern and background for his investigation of natural phenomena. Nature, he declares in a pregnant phrase, is the Art of God (an excellent way, incidentally, of avoiding his natural tendency to slip into pantheism); and all physical phenomena are mere Platonic shadows of ideal and absolute reality. At the highest point of the Ladder is God, with the Angels a little below; at the bottom lie the vegetable and mineral worlds. But in the central position, poised between physical and divine, and partaking of both, stands Man— 'that great and true *Amphibium*', as Browne describes him, 'whose nature is disposed to live, not onely like other creatures in divers elements, but in divided and distinguished worlds'. Browne, in fact, still applied the traditional concept of macrocosm and microcosm to the world; and Man, for him, represents the focal point of potential knowledge:

> Wee carry with us the wonders we seeke without us: There is all *Africa* and her prodigies in us; we are that bold and adventurous piece of nature, which he that studies wisely learnes in a *compendium* what others labour at in a divided piece and endlesse volume.
>
> (*Rel. Med.*, Part I, section 15)

In considering Browne we are all too apt to forget the physician while analysing his faith. At least half Browne's creative mind depends for its conceptual imagery on his medical and scientific awareness; and this awareness often accords more nearly with his notions of universal harmony than we might suppose. He allows his intellect to follow up innumerable isolated phenomena, but carefully avoids co-ordinating his research in the modern sense. This is his method of saving the appearances. He can collect data to his heart's content as long as no dangerous general law is allowed to emerge from his findings: which explains the piecemeal character of much in his work. He resembles in this the victim of the old music-hall joke, who has never seen an inference and therefore cannot draw one.

Thus when he speaks of the 'strange and mystical trans-migrations of silkworms', Browne is, at one level, applying the results (as we know from his notes) of painstaking laboratory observation; but on the higher plane he is shaping the visible manifestation into his *a priori* Platonic scheme of things. For him this implies no inconsistency; he finds no difficulty in accommodating to his religious tenets the scientific *credo* which he lays down in *Christian Morals*:

> Let thy Studies be free as thy Thoughts and Contemplations, but fly not only upon the wings of Imagination; joyn Sense unto Reason, and Experiment unto Speculation, and so give life unto Embryon Truths, and Verities yet in their Chaos. There is nothing more acceptable unto the Ingenious World, than this noble Elucta- tion of Truth; wherein, against the tenacity of Prejudice and Prescription, this Century now prevaileth.

Nor does Browne find any trouble in reconciling this advice (which, within limits, he follows scrupulously him- self) with an acceptance of demonology and witchcraft. To deny the existence of the Devil and his agents is to deny, by implication, the whole of the fixed spiritual hierarchy, and thus lay oneself open to a charge of atheism. Following the same double standard, Browne experiments in detail with the atomic theory, but sternly warns his son, on re- ligious grounds, against reading Lucretius.

It is against this background that Browne's first deliberate venture into the world of authorship must be considered. *Pseudodoxia Epidemica*, commonly known—though not by its author—as *Vulgar Errors*, appeared in 1646, and proved immensely popular during Browne's lifetime. Despite its summary dismissal by modern critics—few of whom appear to have read it with any care—as a jumble of old wive's tales and *idées reçues* culled from the pages of Pliny or Dioscorides, it was planned and executed with a perfectly serious scientific purpose. Far from perpetuating myths, it aimed to remove the worst of those superstitions, irrational fancies, and popular legends then current regarding the natural world; and in the process to deal a blow at the deadening influence of so-called classical 'authorities'.

Unfortunately, of course, Browne had a generous share of all the vices he attacked; he was, besides, severely handicapped by his religious scruples. But the intention was there.

Pseudodoxia Epidemica makes fascinating reading, not only for the devotee of *curiosa*, but also for anyone interested in the popular (as opposed to the 'advanced') beliefs current in the seventeenth century. The sub-titles of sections tell their own story: 'That an Elephant hath no joints'; 'That a Badger hath the Legs of one side shorter than of the other'; 'That Storks will only live in Republicks and free States'; and, with ingenuous honesty, 'Of some Relations whose truth we fear'. But wherever theology permitted, the matter was put to scientific proof: 'That Flos Affricanus is poison, and destroyeth dogs', Browne observes tranquilly, 'in two experiments we have not found'.

The obvious inspiration for a work of this nature is Bacon's *Advancement of Learning*; but Browne's scheme for the extirpation of popular error differs materially from Bacon's Idols. He seems to owe more to the classical tradition of Scepticism. Many of the experiments are surprisingly sound; and Browne's biological observations supply revealing glosses to the imagery of his more literary works. The life-cycle was never far from his mind.

Pseudodoxia Epidemica has suffered neglect for two main reasons. It is scientifically obsolete, and not composed, on the whole, in that heightened mystical style which is the main attraction for Browne's readers today. But the style, plain and serviceable in the main though it be, is still underrated: again and again Browne enriches his text with a memorable phrase or associative image—as when, discussing the properties of crystal, he credits it with 'the seeds of petrification and Gorgon within itself'. And as for the experimental research—the hours spent observing the slow growth of duckweed or foetus, the behaviour of electrified bodies, the swarming creatures gyrating in a drop of rainwater—all this was for Browne simply a physical demonstration of the ideal reality embodied in the ultimate macrocosm. Yet the traffic of suggestion moved in both directions: it seems certain that the miracle of the developing embryo, which so fascinated Browne, also led him to formulate large generalities, by analogy, about the universe.

Browne saw the microcosm in the microscope: throughout his life he preserved a passion for the minute intricacies of the insect or plant world, which he found more to his taste than the Creator's larger and clumsier pieces of handiwork. There is the closest possible inter-relationship between his work in biology, his religious beliefs, his general philosophy, his well-known thematic preoccupations, and his use of metaphor, image and symbol (including his obsession with the mystical numerology of Pythagoreanism and the Cabbala). His literary achievement owes its power, depth and associative richness precisely to this interaction of widely differing modes of apprehension and thought. A stale literary theme is transmuted in Browne's laboratory; his symbols hatch from eggs or frog-spawn to soar into the cosmos, and his mysticism makes poetry of gestation.

Browne, as we might expect, adhered to the 'vitalistic' school of biology, according to which all living creatures shared in a 'vegetal or nutritive soul', the nature of which was akin to fire or light. He also believed in panspermatism, the doctrine which taught that, at the creation, seminal particles were diffused through the world, where they continue to cause generation by direct entry into the organism. After death this 'seminal principle' leaves the corpse and becomes available once more: it is a kind of indestructible *élan vital*.

It is not hard to see how from this pseudo-scientific theory a more general cosmology could be inferred. It was a short step (on the principle, again, of microcosm and macrocosm) from panspermatic vitalism to the divinity of the World Soul; from the unseen nutritive fire to the Invisible Flame of Life. The intersecting point of matter and spirit could be conceived as lying in the generative seminality of the womb: 'Parts of the seed', Browne noted, 'do seem to contain the Idea and power of the whole.' Again, from the human womb an easy transference could be made (with good literary precedent) to Chaos as the Universal Womb; and the departure of the 'seminal principle' at death also fostered a paradoxical connection between the grave and re-birth, this life and the next. Womb and tomb achieved a kind of mystical identity.

Meanwhile, in the womb of Browne's imagination, all these elements slowly fused and germinated. Image, theme and interpretation came together to form a single creative entity; and fifteen years later Browne produced his unquestioned masterpiece.

III

URN AND QUINCUNX

Pseudodoxia Epidemica had appeared in 1646, the year which saw the Parliamentarians' final triumph in the Civil War. *Hydriotaphia*, or *Urn Burial*, and *The Garden of Cyrus* were published, together, in 1658—the year of Cromwell's death. Thus the gestation of the later works coincided almost exactly with the Protectorate; and this is not without its significance. Browne was an ardent Royalist in a town that favoured the Protector: his political views probably underlay his one marked intolerance, for:

> that great enemy of reason, vertue and religion, the multitude; that numerous piece of monstrosity, which taken asunder seeme men, and the reasonable creatures of God; but confused together, make but one great beast, and a monstrosity more prodigious than Hydra. (*Rel. Med.* Part II, section 1)

During the whole of those fifteen years he must have been under very violent emotional and psychological stress.

He did not, as is so often supposed, withdraw himself in Epicurean isolation: as his letters show, he took a keen interest in politics and world affairs. Nothing could be further from the truth than the popular conception of

Browne as a shy, solitary, unworldly recluse. To the end of his life he remained a practising physician, in close contact (if any man was) with the intimate realities of birth, suffering, and death.

It was a century, too, when death was cheap, and *memento mori* stamped on all men's minds. Battle and famine raged through the land; plague and syphilis were perennial visitors. The graveyard temper which these conditions engendered was hardly lightened by gloomy Calvinist talk of predestination and hell-fire. From the Jacobean dramatists onwards, grisly symbols of charnel corruption and morbid psychology formed an integral element in every seventeenth-century writer's creative equipment; and Browne, notoriously, had his full share of them.

His obsession with death wavers between fear and desire. A cancelled[1] passage preserved in two manuscripts of the *Religio Medici* is revealing: 'It is a symptom of melancholy to be afraid of death, yet sometimes to desire it; this latter I have often discovered in my selfe, and thinke no man ever desired life, as I have sometimes death.' And again: 'For the world, I count it not an Inne, but an Hospitall, and a place, not to live, but to die in.' Where he differs from, say, Donne, is in his medical detachment from the physical unpleasantness of death: he never flinches in mere horror or nausea. He is not immune, even, from hard-boiled medical jokes: 'Death hath spurs', he remarks in the *Pseudodoxia*, 'and carcasses have been courted.'

Vitalistic biology, Fideism, embryology, antiquarianism; mystical numerology, the precepts of Pythagoras and the Cambridge Platonists; Dante's Paradisal vision, Gnostic eschatology, the mediaeval hierarchy, microcosm and macrocosm; the ravages of disease and civil war, the ubiquitous signs of transient mortality—all these passed through the creative alembic of Browne's mind to produce that single immortal volume. There has been a fashion among

[1] Denonain (p. 51) prints this passage in Part I, section 38, as an integral part of the established text.

modern critics to study *Hydriotaphia* and *The Garden of Cyrus* as though they were separate, independent works. In fact—as Browne himself makes clear—they form a single, indivisible unity:

> That we conjoyn these parts of different Subjects, or that this [*The Garden of Cyrus*] should succeed the other; Your judgement will admit without impute of incongruity; Since the delightfull World comes after death, and Paradise succeeds the Grave. Since the verdant state of things is the Symbole of the Resurrection, and to flourish in the state of Glory, we must first be sown in corruption. Beside the ancient practise of Noble Persons, to conclude in Garden-Graves, and Urnes themselves of old, to be wrapt up in flowers and garlands.

These two essays, then, are in structure an echo of Dante; they form Browne's *Purgatorio* and *Paradiso*.

The symbolic framework chosen to sustain such a meditation is curious in every sense of the word. *Hydriotaphia* ostensibly discusses a cache of ancient burial-urns unearthed at Old Walsingham; *The Garden of Cyrus* revolves round the various aspects of the quincunx—five points arranged in such a way (:·:) that, connected, they form an X, or Greek *Chi*. Again, Browne makes an explicit statement as to the reason for going at his theme in such an odd way:

> In this multiplicity of writing, bye and barren Themes are best fitted for invention; Subjects so often discoursed confine the Imagination, and fix our conceptions unto the notions of fore-writers. Beside, such Discourses allow excursions, and venially admit of collaterall truths, though at some distance from their principals.

By concentrating, almost like a hypnotist, on this pair of unfamiliar symbols, Browne paradoxically releases the reader's mind into an infinite number of associative levels of awareness, without any preconceptions. Emphasis on particularities gives shape and substance to quite literally cosmic generalizations.

Both essays are constructed according to the same formula: four chapters of examples and instances, much in the tradition of the *Pseudodoxia* (types of burial, categories of urn, variations on the quincuncial pattern) rise cumulatively to a fifth, in which theme and variations are gathered up and resolved in an exalted climax, a mystical and poetic *O altitudo*. The two works are interlinked by a dualistic pattern of opposed symbols—death and life, body and soul, substance and form, accident and design, time and space, darkness and light, earth and heaven. They can no more be separated than the voices of a fugue: taken together they form one of the deepest, most complex, most symbolically pregnant statements ever composed on the great double theme of mortality and eternity.

We feel the shadow of devouring Time fall across every page. *Fugit hora*: 'our Fathers finde their graves in our short memories . . . old Families last not three Oaks'. Vanity of vanities, all is vanity, and mere human attempts to achieve immortality are doomed to ludicrous failure. Browne foreshadows the lesson of Shelley's *Ozymandias*:

> The iniquity of oblivion blindely scattereth her poppy, and deals with the memory of men without distinction to merit of perpetuity. Who can but pity the founder of the Pyramids? *Herostratus* lives that burnt the Temple of *Diana*, he is almost lost that built it; Time hath spared the Epitaph of *Adrians* horse, confounded that of himself. In vain we compute our felicities by the advantage of our good names, since bad have equall durations; and *Thersites* is like to live as long as *Agamemnon*. . . . Without the favour of the everlasting Register the first man had been as unknown as the last, and *Methuselah's* long life had been his only Chronicle. . . .
>
> Man is a Noble Animal, splendid in ashes, and pompous in the grave, solemnizing Nativities and Deaths with equall lustre, nor omitting Ceremonies of bravery, in the infamy of his nature.
>
> (*Hydriotaphia*, ch. 5)

Mere human knowledge, too, is a poor and pitiful substitute for divine reality. Browne's parade of dubious antiquarian knowledge in *Hydriotaphia* seems almost designed to highlight the futility of scholarship. 'Than the time of these Urnes deposited', he admits, 'or precise Antiquity of these Reliques nothing of more uncertainty'—and underlines the point by identifying obviously Saxon pots as Roman. He had (as is often forgotten) already delivered a scathing verdict on the value of antiquities generally, in the *Religio Medici*.

Throughout the *Hydriotaphia* (as Mr. F. L. Huntley has pointed out in a brilliant essay) the subject remains 'small, temporal, local, *sui generis*, mutable, pathetic, nameless'—in sharp contrast to the soaring eternal universalities of *The Garden of Cyrus*:

> But these are sad and sepulchral Pitchers, which have no joyful voices; silently expressing old mortality, the ruines of forgotten times, and can only speak with life, how long in this corruptible frame, some parts may be uncorrupted.

Yet the burial-urn, the symbol of death, is also the symbol of birth. Browne's practised medical eye at once saw its odd resemblance to the human womb:

> The common form with necks was a proper figure, making our last bed like our first; nor much unlike the Urnes of our Nativity, while we lay in the nether part of the Earth, and inward vault of our Microcosme....

In the final chapter this cosmo-biological conceit is given a fresh twist: 'Death', Browne writes, 'must be the Lucina of life.' As the seminal particles leave the dead body and enter the living, so the grave itself becomes the womb of our re-birth. Here is the vital connecting image between the two essays, the bridge leading from mortality to eternity. Thus the doctrine of panspermatism is transformed into Christian eschatology:

> Life is a pure flame, and we live by an invisible Sun within us....
> And if any have been so happy as truly to understand Christian annihilation, extasis, exolution, liquefaction, transformation, the kisse of the Spouse, gustation of God, and ingression into the divine shadow, they have already had an handsome anticipation of heaven; the glory of the world is surely over, and the earth in ashes unto them.
> To subsist in lasting Monuments, to live in their productions, to

exist in their names, and praedicament of *Chymera's*, was large satisfaction unto old expectations and made one part of their *Elyziums*. But all this is nothing in the Metaphysicks of true belief...

When we turn from Urn to Quincunx, from rational to mystical apprehension of reality, the tone insensibly changes. Though the quincuncial figure is used (as the urns were) as a kind of hieroglyph, which enables the reader to grasp its several aspects simultaneously, the method of development pursues a Platonic rather than an Aristotelian course. We first consider 'artificial' manifestations of the Quincunx—that is, man's use of the figure in imitation of Nature; next, Nature's own quincuncial phenomena; lastly, the 'mystical' prototype—the Idea or Form of Quincunciality in the Creator's mind.

As to the reason for Browne's having chosen this particular symbol and no other in such a context, a clue is to be found in that passage where he discusses the related Platonic emblem of the two circles bisecting one another at right angles. Mr. Huntley interprets the meaning of this emblem as follows:

> The circle is God, perfection, immortality; the horizontal that crosses the circle represents the corporal, divisible, death; where the two lines meet we perceive the 'mystical' decussation, the cross, or quincunxial [*sic*] figure, i.e. the systasis of the main opposition between 'death' and 'life'.

Seen from one angle, that is, the intersecting circles appear as a cross, thus: +. If they are then rotated through 90° on a vertical axis they will be changed into the Greek θ, *Theta*, standing for *Thanatos* or Death.

Mystical symbolism of this kind is woven throughout the texture of Browne's work and adds, often subconsciously, to its associative power of impact. Only a highly superficial critic[1] could ever have described *The Garden of Cyrus* as 'about as nondescript a piece of Pythagorean madness as ever bewildered the wits of man'. It is anything but nondescript;

[1] Paul Elmer More, p. 158: See Bibliography.

there is nothing vague or woolly about Browne's mysticism, any more than Pascal's. Every symbol is interrelated with the over-all pattern—'according to the ordainer of order and mysticall Mathematicks of the City of Heaven'.

The development of *The Garden of Cyrus* is in one sense closely parallel to the ascent of the Ladder of Being. Browne's early examples are chosen from man-made gardens, his next from natural growth; he closes with the Quincunx of Heaven itself. Gardens suggest the additional symbolism of Paradise; natural growth allows an organic digression into embryology and theories of generation. Just as *Hydriotaphia* smells of darkness, death, the futility of human endeavour when Man attempts to stand alone (at one level it could be read as an epitaph on the angry dead of the civil and religious wars) so *The Garden of Cyrus* is irradiated with the symbols of growth and fertility: it is seminal in every sense, flooded with physical and spiritual light.

But Browne's favourite, all-embracing metaphor is that of the circle (everything, from God to the revolutions of the arterial blood, he somehow subordinated to the circular concept) and his paradisal picture does not remain in a static blaze of unchanging glory. Neither as biologist, astronomer, mystic nor artist could he allow this. The wheel of time must turn, the circle of generation must proceed. Even eternity has its seasons: the darkness of death is also the darkness of life, as night follows day:

> But Seeds themselves do lie in perpetual shades, either under the leaf, or shut up in coverings; And such as lye barest, have their husks, skins, and pulps about them, wherein the nebbe and generative particle lyeth moist and secured from the injury of Ayre and Sunne. Darknesse and light hold interchangeable dominions, and alternately rule the seminal state of things. Light unto *Pluto* is darknesse unto *Jupiter*. Legions of seminal *Idaea's* lie in their second Chaos and *Orcus of Hipocrates;* till putting on the habits of their forms, they show themselves upon the stage of the world, and open dominion of *Jove.* . . . Life it self is but the shadow of death, and souls departed but the shadows of the living: All things fall under this name. The

> Sunne it self is but the dark *simulachrum*, and light but the shadow
> of God.   (*Garden of Cyrus*, ch. 4)

So on the drowsy, opiate stroke of midnight ('To keep our
eyes open longer were but to act our Antipodes') *The Garden
of Cyrus* draws to a muted, *andante* close. With *Hydriotaphia* it
indeed fulfils a theme, as Browne put it, 'not impertinent unto
our profession, whose study is life and death'; and—quite
incidentally, one suspects, from the author's viewpoint—
crystallizes that theme in language and imagery which have
seldom been matched in the English language.

Browne's other works may be briefly mentioned here.
A Letter To a Friend—probably composed in 1656, and not,
as generally supposed, 1672, and therefore in one sense a
preliminary study for *Hydriotaphia*—is an idiosyncratic
exercise in that familiar form, the *consolatio*. A young patient
under Browne's care had recently died, of tuberculosis;
the friend is treated to a clinical account of his death, and a
homily on how to live. *Christian Morals*, the product of
Browne's old age, is a collection of rigid if illuminating
aphorisms, variously described as 'sermonettes on the
conduct of life', 'a collection of the noblest thoughts, drest
in the uncouthest language possible', and 'an elaborate and
magnificent parody of the Book of Proverbs': it shows—
despite some brilliant flashes in Browne's old style—how
age had formalized and stereotyped his talents.

The list is rounded off with a collection of miscellaneous
scholarly tracts, chiefly remarkable for the light they shed on
Browne's exceedingly wide interests: these ranged from
ornithology to comparative linguistics. But he will remain,
for future generations, one of those rare and special writers
whose whole creative effort was crystallized and subsumed
in two or three slender volumes. The two essays of 1658 are
the focal point for a mind which may properly be compared
with that both of Coleridge and Leonardo da Vinci.

WHAT SONG THE SYRENS SANG

Though he subsequently became the favourite of literary
men, such as Hazlitt, Lamb, or Stevenson, Sir Thomas
Browne himself never made any claim to be a man of letters
(in the modern sense). He actually expressed the opinion—
and repeated it—that 'it were no loss like that of Galen's
library if these [i.e. poets and 'poetical' writers generally]
had found the same fate; and would in some way requite
the neglect of solid Authors, if they were less pursued'.
The attitude to 'fiction' is Platonic; the solidly professional
motive is very much Browne's own. Some critics, finding
this hard to swallow, have made great play with a dozen or
two works of English literature found in the catalogue of
Browne's library; but they omit to mention the two
thousand other volumes, in four or five languages, on medicine, theology, physics, mathematics, biology and travel.
Browne's was primarily a working library.

Clearly he *did* read pure literature; but it most often seems
to have been with an ulterior end in view. We have already
seen the debt he owed to Dante. He was too, exceedingly
well read in the classics, both Greek and Latin; yet though,
inevitably, his own work was permeated by classical in-
fluences of style, cadence, language and thought, he did not
appear to read ancient authors so much for aesthetic satis-
tion as for factual information. His attitude to the classics
(despite the *Pseudodoxia*) is comparable to his attitude to
Holy Writ: the main object in view seems to be the citation
of chapter and verse on controversial issues. Browne was
not, and never pretended to be, a professional *littérateur*—a
fact which saved him from many literary vices. His wide
reading was largely technical, and he achieved the final
chapters of *Hydriotaphia* and *The Garden of Cyrus*, one
suspects, in much the same tranced condition as Coleridge
composing Kubla Khan. (Despite the polished state of
the published version, early drafts in the British Museum

confirm this suspicion. The pen is driven across the page in a white-hot, illegible frenzy, scarce able to keep up with the succession of thoughts and images that crowded into the author's mind.)

The comparison with Coleridge is a generally profitable one. Both were obsessed by dream-imagery and dream-symbolism. Both, in their finest work, display an exactly analogous process of absorption and crystallization. (Did Browne possibly take laudanum? It seems very likely. He had free access to drugs, and used opiates in various experiments.) Both were widely read in non-literary sources, travel-books in particular, and had strong scientific interests. Browne took his original material on the quincunx, for example, from two excessively dry Italian treatises on agriculture. One of these gave him the notion of Nature's domination by the quincuncial figure, and his imagination used this supposition as a spring-board into the cosmos.

Browne had an extremely well-stocked mind, but took little account of his immediate literary predecessors. No one, as an American scholar remarked despairingly, has yet discovered a model for the *Hydriotaphia*. All this explains both Browne's strength and his weaknesses. He was honestly indifferent to literary art as an end in itself; he lacked (except in a metaphysical sense) any architectonic imagination on the large scale—his basic unit always remained the commonplace-book citation; he was a busy practising doctor, and his medical duties absorbed the bulk of his creative energies. But his profession was also his strength in that it offered his creative imagination an abundance of raw material to work on. His mystical reverence for the processes of life and death was reinforced by his scientific awareness of these processes in every minuscule detail: it is symbolically appropriate that in his numerical meditations on the quincunx he should also embody a vital botanical principle—the quinary arrangement of leaves.

Two basic literary sources did, however, have a vast influence on Browne's prose: Latin oratory and the Authorized Version. From the first he borrowed, among other things, his *clausulae*—those superbly rhythmic sentence-endings which appear whenever his subject-matter heightens in intensity,[1] echoes of Cicero and Seneca. 'Pyramids, arches, obelisks, were but the irregularities of vainglory, and wild enormities of ancient magnanimity'; '. . . and cannot excusably decline the consideration of that duration, which maketh Pyramids pillars of snow, and all that's past a moment'; or, perhaps most striking of all—to complete an earlier quotation:

> Life is a pure flame, and we live by an invisible Sun within us. A small fire sufficeth for life, great flames seemed too little after death, while men vainly affected precious pyres, and to burn like *Sardanapalus;* but the wisedom of funerall Laws found the folly of prodigall blazes, and reduced undoing fires unto the rule of sober obsequies, wherein few could be so mean as not to provide wood, pitch, a mourner, and an Urne. (*Hydriotaphia,* ch. 5)

The five-beat rhythm predominates at moments of greatest intensity; and perhaps it is not fanciful to suppose (as Basil Anderton did) that this, too, can be related to the ubiquitous quincuncial pattern.

Perhaps Browne's greatest single debt, however, is to the Authorized Version, both in language, imagery, and cadence. From the Book of Proverbs he acquired the habit of making pregnant aphorisms—a trait especially apparent in *Christian Morals.* From the Book of Psalms he borrowed the Hebrew device of antiphonal statement—the repetition that is of the sense of a phrase in different terms. With Browne this involved juxtaposing Latinate and Anglo-Saxon vocabulary—another exercise in fugal contrasts: 'Chaos of preordination and night of their forebeings'; 'Areopagy and dark Tribunal of our Hearts'; or, in a slightly different but

---

[1] Sir Herbert Read observed memorably of prose style that 'it is born, not with the words, but with the thought, and with whatever confluence of instincts and emotions the thought is accompanied'—a statement peculiarly applicable to Browne.

no less striking contrast, 'To well manage our Affections and Wild Horses of Plato'.

Browne's heavy use of classical loan-words (what Coleridge called his 'hyperlatinism') has an exceedingly far-reaching effect on his symbolism as well as the texture of his prose. There are whole centuries of associative meaning contained in the well-placed Latinate term. For obvious historical reasons many classical words, with their factual allusiveness and rich verbal harmonics, carry plangent overtones and echoes which our bare Anglo-Saxon could never achieve. Browne, in fact, is once again employing hieroglyphs, this time in a linguistic sense, to pack his prose with as much concentrated symbolic meaning as it will stand: he turns, instinctively, to the poetic method. As with Milton, this is most immediately appreciable in his skilful use of proper names. Janus, Alcmena, Pythagoras, Osiris: their significance germinates and expands in the reader's mind like an opening seed:

> But in this latter Scene of time we cannot expect such Mummies unto our memories, when ambition may fear the Prophecy of *Elias*, and *Charles* the fifth can never hope to live within two *Methusela's* of *Hector*.   (*Hydriotaphia*, ch. 5)

What saves Browne's prose-style and imagery from the Euphuistic excesses that ruined so many other writers drawing on similar sources? Primarily, perhaps, the tension constantly generated between his scientific intellect and his artistic imagination, his sensuous feeling for words and the religious austerity of his subject-matter. (The same phenomenon may be observed later in Hopkins.) Browne never lets his style run away with his sense, never writes ornamental Latinate prose for the mere pleasure of achieving an *unrelated* verbal effect or paradoxical humour. Sometimes he writes purely as a scientist, sometimes as scientist and artist together; but never as artist alone. In his letters, and for the bulk of the *Pseudodoxia*, he writes a plain, serviceable, functional prose: this has disconcerted some of his aesthetic admirers,[1] who apparently expected him to write in a perpetual state of exaltation. But Browne's type of inspirational flash-point is reached, with luck, twice in a life-time; Coleridge wrote only one *Kubla Khan*, and Traherne, in all the *Centuries of Meditation*, never recaptured the mescalinate ecstasy of his 'orient and immortal wheat'.

This is not to suggest that Browne did not have a superb natural ear for rhythm and language: he obviously did. (By the same token, as an auditory type he is markedly deficient in visual imagery.) Many of the words he coined have stuck in the language: *hallucination, umbrella, medical, antediluvian, opaline*, and, ironically enough, *literary*. But the instinct to form neologisms is due as much to a need for scientific terminology as a vigorous imagination: we are not so conversant with some of his other, more technical inventions: *stillicidious, chylifactive*, the weird *retromingent*.

It is noticeable that Browne's hypnotic, incantatory effect, which we associate with his highest flights of prose, is generally accompanied by a slight blurring of mental focus, what one critic sourly characterized as 'a certain ambiguity or recalcitrant recession of sense, of the sort that we normally associate with poetry'. At the same time the imagery achieves a peak of fragmentary, dream-like allusiveness which reminds us of De Quincey rather than Coleridge, and we remember that drugs can be soporific as well as stimulating:

> But the Quincunx of Heaven runs low, and 'tis time to close the five ports of knowledge; We are unwilling to spin out our awaking thoughts into the phantasmes of sleep, which too often continueth praecogitations; making Cables of Cobwebbes and Wildernesses of handsome Groves. Beside, *Hippocrates* hath spoke so little, and the Oneirocriticall Masters have left such frigid Interpretations from plants, that there is little encouragement to dream of Paradise it self. Nor will the sweetest delight of Gardens afford much comfort in sleep; wherein the dulnesse of that sense shakes hands with delectable odours; and though in the Bed of *Cleopatra*, can hardly with any delight raise up the ghost of a Rose.   (*Garden of Cyrus*, Ch. 5)

[1] cf. Prof. Austin Warren, pp. 678–9. See Bibliography.

If we shake ourselves into wakefulness, we realize that those superb final lines merely mean that you cannot smell flowers when you are asleep; but poppy-and-mandragora confidence tricks have by then been worked on our imaginations. The Coleridgean dream-symbolism has quietly invaded that no-man's-land where science, theology and imagination meet, and alchemized them into something rich and strange —yet familiar as an echo. A point is reached where the meaning, as in all lyrical poetry, cannot be divorced from the words: the words *are* the meaning.

Sir Thomas Browne is his own most fascinating subject of study, and knows it:

> That world which I regard is my selfe; it is the Microcosme of mine owne frame that I cast mine eye on; for the other, I use it but like my Globe, and turne it round sometimes for my recreation.
>
> (*Rel. Med.* Part II, section 11)

His antiquarian tinge of mind and his obsessional devotion to serious study recall that prodigious Roman polymath, the Elder Pliny. His personal temperament, however, remains quintessentially English: ironic, melancholy, learned, humorous,[1] eccentric, he is, as Leslie Stephen remarked, Uncle Toby and Mr. Shandy rolled into one. But at a deeper level, his extraordinary use of birth-death, light-dark, growth-decay imagery, and the intense religious love suffusing all his work with a reverent tenderness for created life—these look forward strikingly to a Bible-cadenced modern poet who also composed in love of Man and in praise of God. It might have been of Browne that Dylan Thomas wrote:

> The lips of time leech to the fountain head;
> Love drips and gathers, but the fallen blood

---

[1] In *Pseudodoxia Epidemica* he remarks drily: 'We shall not, I hope, disparage the Resurrection of our Redeemer, if we say the Sun doth not dance on Easter day.'

Shall calm her sores.
And I am dumb to tell a weather's wind
How time has ticked a heaven round the stars.

In that stanza we can trace the whole paradigm of Sir
Thomas Browne's creative achievement, and the whole
quality of his faith.

SIR THOMAS BROWNE

A Select Bibliography

(Place of publication London, unless stated otherwise.)

Bibliographies:

A BIBLIOGRAPHY OF SIR THOMAS BROWNE, KT., M.D., by G. L. Keynes. Cambridge (1924).

A FRENCH BIBLIOGRAPHY OF SIR THOMAS BROWNE, by O. Leroy. Paris (1931).

Collected Works:

THE WORKS (1685–6).

Contains little of the posthumous work, and none of the Correspondence.

THE WORKS, edited by S. Wilkin, 4 vols. (1833–6).

The first critical edition, which laid the foundations for all future work. It includes Johnson's *Life*, a Supplementary Memoir by Wilkin which draws on much primary MS. material, many additional opuscula, and the bulk of the Correspondence.

THE WORKS, edited by C. E. Sayle, 3 vols. (1904–7).

Textually unreliable and omits the Correspondence, but makes use for the first time of the author-annotated copy of *Hydriotaphia* at Trinity College, Cambridge.

THE WORKS, edited by G. L. Keynes, 6 vols. (1928–31).

Vols. 5 and 6, *Miscellaneous Works* and *Correspondence*, reprinted with corrections, 1946. This, the standard edition, adds further to the Correspondence, and revises Wilkin's text at many points, from MSS. in the British Museum and the Bodleian. The transcription, especially of passages in Latin, is uneven. The editions of Carter and Denonain (see below) now supersede Keynes's text for *Religio Medici*, *Hydriotaphia* and *The Garden of Cyrus*.

Separate Works:

RELIGIO MEDICI (1642).

See 'The First Edition of *Religio Medici*' in *Harvard Library Bulletin*, II, 1948, for an authoritative ruling on the priority and status of the two editions (one of them pirated) of 1642 and 1643 respectively. The most valuable critical editions are those by W. A. Greenhill, 1881; W. Murison, Cambridge, 1922; and J. J. Denonain, Cambridge, 2nd ed., revised 1955.

PSEUDODOXIA EPIDEMICA (1646)

No separate modern edition.

HYDRIOTAPHIA AND THE GARDEN OF CYRUS (1658).

Modern critical editions include those by Sir J. Evans, 1893 (*Hydriotaphia* only); W. A. Greenhill, 1896; W. Murison, Cambridge, 1922 (*Hydriotaphia* only); and J. Carter, 1932 (limited edition), 2nd ed., revised, Cambridge, 1958.

MISCELLANY TRACTS (1683).

Edited by Archbishop Tenison. No separate modern edition.

A LETTER TO A FRIEND (1690).

No modern separate edition, but reprinted in Greenhill's edition of *Religio Medici*, 1881, and in the Everyman edition of *Religio Medici*, edited by C. H. Herford.

POSTHUMOUS WORKS (1712).

Superseded by Wilkin and Keynes.

CHRISTIAN MORALS, edited by J. Jeffery, Arch-Deacon of Norwich. Cambridge [1716].

Modern editions include Greenhill's, 1881, and that of S. C. Roberts, Cambridge, 1927.

Some Critical and Biographical Studies:

Note: There are few good books on Sir Thomas Browne, those by Leroy, Dunn and Merton (see below) being the best of a surprisingly poor field. The specialist must consult the learned journals for any satisfactory up-to-date treatment of him.

OBSERVATIONS UPON 'RELIGIO MEDICI', by Sir K. Digby (1643).

MEDICUS MEDICATUS, &c., by A. Ross (1645).

ARCANA MICROCOSMI, &c., by A. Ross (1651).

These two tracts represent the extreme, almost lunatic fringe of theological conservatism; Ross was largely responsible for Browne's reputation as an atheist.

LIFE OF SIR THOMAS BROWNE, by S. Johnson (1756).

HOURS IN A LIBRARY, by L. Stephen, 2nd series (1876).

APPRECIATIONS, by W. Pater (1899).

SIR THOMAS BROWNE: AN APPRECIATION, by A White, D.D. Edinburgh (1898).

PURITAN AND ANGLICAN, by E. Dowden (1900).

SIR THOMAS BROWNE, by E. Gosse (1905).

Superficial and often inaccurate, but the first attempt at a critical biography since Dr. Johnson's.

STUDIES OF RELIGIOUS DUALISM, by P. E. More, 6th series. Cambridge, Mass. (1909).

Shelburne Essays.

SIR THOMAS BROWNES 'RELIGIO MEDICI': EIN VERSCHOLLENES DENKMAL DES ENGLISCHEN DEISMUS, &c. von W. Schonack. Tübingen (1911).

One of the first attempts to place Browne's religious thought in its proper historical context.

ESSAYS IN BIOGRAPHY, by C. Whibley (1913).

SKETCHES FROM A LIBRARY WINDOW, by B. Anderton. Cambridge (1922).

Contains an excellent preliminary investigation of Browne's prose rhythms.

BOOKS AND CHARACTERS FRENCH AND ENGLISH, by L. Strachey (1922).

'Sir Thomas Browne', by J. A. Symonds, in *Modern English Essays*, Vol. 3, 1922.

OUTFLYING PHILOSOPHY, by R. Sencourt. Hildesheim (1924).

A suggestive but chronically inaccurate study of Browne's religious thought, especially in relation to his knowledge of Aquinas.

SIR THOMAS BROWNE, HIS SKULL, PORTRAITS, AND ANCESTORS, by M. L. Tildesley (1927).

LE CHEVALIER THOMAS BROWNE: 1605–82; SA VIE, SA PENSÉE, ET SON ART, par O. Leroy. Paris (1931).

THE GREAT AMPHIBIUM, by J. Needham (1931).

'Sir Thomas Browne and his Reading', by R. R. Cawley, in *Publ. of the Modern Lang. Assoc. of America*, Vol. 48/1, 1933.

THE SEVENTEENTH-CENTURY BACKGROUND, by B. Willey (1934).

'Hydriotaphia', by J. N. Cline, in *Five Studies in Literature*: Univ. of California. Publ. in English, Vol. 8. 1940.

'Early Drafts of *The Garden of Cyrus*', by J. S. Finch, in *Publ. of the Mod. Lang. Assoc. of America*, Vol. 55/2, 1940.

'Browne and the Quincunx', by J. S. Finch, in *Studies in Philology*, Vol. 37, 1940.

IN DIVIDED AND DISTINGUISHED WORLDS, by D. K. Ziegler. Cambridge, Mass. (1944).

Attempts to show that Browne kept his scientific and religious concepts separate: stimulating but improbable.

ENGLISH NATURALISTS, by C. E. Raven. Cambridge (1947).

'Browne and the Genesis of Paradox', by M. L. Wiley, in *Journal of the History of Ideas*, Vol. 9, 1948.

SCIENCE AND IMAGINATION IN SIR THOMAS BROWNE, by E. S. Merton. New York (1949).

SIR THOMAS BROWNE: A STUDY IN RELIGIOUS PHILOSOPHY, by W. P. Dunn. 2nd edition, Minneapolis (1950).

SIR THOMAS BROWNE: A DOCTOR'S LIFE OF SCIENCE AND FAITH, by J. S. Finch. New York (1950).

The only biography in English since Gosse's; is 'popular' and disappointingly lightweight.

'*Hydriotaphia* and *The Garden of Cyrus:* A Paradox and a Cosmic Vision', etc., by M. A. Heideman, in *University of Toronto Quarterly*, Vol. 19, 1950.

'The Style of Browne', by A. Warren, in *Kenyon Review*, Vol. 13, 1951.

'Sir Thomas Browne and the Metaphor of the Circle', by F. L. Huntley, in *Journal of the History of Ideas*, Vol. 14, 1953.

'Sir Thomas Browne: The Relationship of *Urn Burial* and *The Garden of Cyrus*', by F. L. Huntley, in *Studies in Philology*, Vol. 53, 1956. The most fruitful single piece of criticism on Browne's work.

EVERY MAN A PHOENIX: STUDIES IN SEVENTEENTH CENTURY AUTO-BIOGRAPHY, by M. Bottrall (1958).

Includes a discussion of *Religio Medici* considered as an autobiographical document.

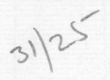